Rufus T Bear's First Reading Book

By Tagore Ramoutar

I like red cars.

A red car.

I like blue cars.

A blue car.

I like police cars.

A police car.

I like fire engines.

A fire engine.

I like trucks.

A truck.

I like red buses.

A red bus.

I like planes.

A plane.

I like fighter planes.

A fighter plane.

I like helicopters.

A helicopter.

I like tanks.

A tank.

I like pirate ships.

A pirate ship.

I like fast trains.

A fast train.

I really like old trains.

A train engine.

I really like diggers.

A digger.

I love tractors!

A tractor.

But a police tractor is even better!

How amazing!

www.ingramcontent.com/pod-product-compliance
Lightning Source LLC
Chambersburg PA
CBHW042105040426
42448CB00002B/143